WORRY
The Joy Stealer

JUNE HUNT

AspirePress

Worry: The Joy Stealer
©2021 Hope For The Heart

Published by Aspire Press
An imprint of Tyndale House Ministries
Carol Stream, Illinois
www.hendricksonrose.com

ISBN 9781628629842

The views and opinions expressed in this book are those of the author(s) and do not necessarily express the views of Rose Publishing, nor is this book intended to be a substitute for mental health treatment or professional counseling. The information in this resource is intended as guidelines for healthy living. Please consult qualified medical, legal, pastoral, and psychological professionals regarding individual concerns.

Cover photo: Sasin Paraksa/Shutterstock.com

Unless otherwise indicated, all Scripture quotations are taken from the Holy Bible, New International Version®, NIV®. Copyright © 1973, 1978, 1984, 2011 by Biblica, Inc.™ Used by permission of Zondervan. All rights reserved worldwide. www.zondervan.com The "NIV" and "New International Version" are trademarks registered in the United States Patent and Trademark Office by Biblica, Inc.™ Scripture quotations marked (ESV) are taken from The ESV® Bible (The Holy Bible, English Standard Version®), copyright © 2001 by Crossway, a publishing ministry of Good News Publishers. Used by permission. All rights reserved. Good News Translation (GNT) in Today's English Version- Second Edition Copyright © 1992 by American Bible Society. Used by Permission. GOD'S WORD (GW) is a copyrighted work of God's Word to the Nations. Quotations are used by permission. Copyright 1995 by God's Word to the Nations. All rights reserved. Scripture quotations marked (MSG) are taken from THE MESSAGE, copyright © 1993, 2002, 2018 by Eugene H. Peterson. Used by permission of NavPress. All rights reserved. Represented by Tyndale House Publishers, a Division of Tyndale House Ministries. Scripture quotations marked (NCV) are taken from the New Century Version®. Copyright © 2005 by Thomas Nelson. Used by permission. All rights reserved. Scripture quotations marked (NKJV) are taken from the New King James Version®. Copyright © 1982 by Thomas Nelson. Used by permission. All rights reserved. Scripture quotations marked (NLT) are taken from the Holy Bible, New Living Translation, copyright © 1996, 2004, 2015 by Tyndale House Foundation. Used by permission of Tyndale House Publishers, Inc., Carol Stream, Illinois 60188. All rights reserved.

For more information on Hope For The Heart, visit www.hopefortheheart.org or call 1-800-488-HOPE (4673).

Printed in the United States of America
020821VP

CONTENTS

Dear friend,

When I was a young girl, I had an uncle whose name was Charles Lake. It was always fun being around Uncle Charlie, not just because he married my aunt Swann which made her Swann Lake (it's true!), but also because he would let me sit on his lap. Uncle Charlie had a Santa-size tummy and would laugh a lot. Better yet, as I sat on his lap he would let me comb his hair … to the right … to the left … all the way back … all the way forward. He would let me comb at will and never really seemed to mind. But perhaps the most important thing to me was that Uncle Charlie gave me attention.

One day, he called our home and invited me to visit him in Shreveport, Louisiana, where he lived. He told me he wanted to take me fishing. Oh, how excited I was. I remember getting on the bus to Shreveport filled with anticipation and looking forward to this new adventure.

Uncle Charlie informed me when I arrived that we would have to get up early in the morning (it was actually more like the middle of the night—and still very dark outside) for our fishing expedition. It was about four in the morning when we rolled out of the driveway and set off to the Lake of the Pines.

I had been fishing before—a few times at White Rock Lake in Dallas—where we used cane poles and chunks of hot dogs for bait stuck on hooks. Frankly, I don't ever remember getting a nibble—not even once. (Obviously, fish don't feel the same way about hot dogs that kids do.) But we thought we were fishing and thoroughly enjoyed the experience.

Uncle Charlie knew a whole lot more about fishing than I'd experienced up to that point. In fact, he provided me with my own rod and reel the day we went fishing. His first words of instruction to me were, "Cast your line." Then he told me that there were certain places (especially around stumps and trees) where the fish liked to swim in and out.

The first time I tried to cast my line, it barely went out three feet. Then Uncle Charlie told me as he showed me, "Make an arc!" So I tried ... and tried, and tried. With each cast and every improved arc, my line went farther and farther out. In time, what I discovered was that part of the secret to good casting is having a little metal weight on the far end of the line, close to the hook. I noticed that when Uncle Charlie cast he would say, "I am going to put it out there." Then he'd point to a particular place and "splash," the line would land in the exact place Uncle Charlie cast it every time. I thought, *How did he do that?*

His next instruction to me was "Reel in your line very slowly." After several hours of casting and reeling, I was really getting the hang of it. In fact, I was plumb proud of myself because I could arc that line and direct my cast—and, boy, was it fun!

Interestingly, the Bible uses the word *cast* in 1 Peter 5:7 where it says, *"Cast all of your cares upon Him for He cares for you."* That's what we're to do—cast, not keep our cares close to us, not place them next to us, but cast them knowing where we are casting them. Similar to a fishing rig, there's a "weight." In real life, the weights (cares) we carry are often incredibly heavy. Think of the last time you carried a weight (burden) that seemed unbearable. God wants you to know that He understands just how heavy your weights are and He asks, "Are you ready to let me carry your wearying weights for you?"

In Matthew 11:29, Jesus tells us, *"Take my yoke upon you and learn from me, for I am gentle and humble in heart, and you will find rest for your souls."* Jesus wants to be yoked with us so that He can carry our weights—so He can bear our burdens. He will make our burdens light. The word, *care*, used in 1 Peter 5, actually means "a distracting care." In the Greek, when it says to *cast*, it means "to throw upon, to deposit once and for all."

Next time a wearisome worry weighs you down, deposit that worry—deposit that distracting care. Make a commitment to give the Lord every concern—everything that would otherwise keep you in a state of restless anxiousness. No, you can't avoid having the weights, but what you do with them is what is all-important. Cast your cares in God's direction today. *"Cast your cares on the Lord and he will sustain you"* (Psalm 55:22).

Yours in the Lord's hope,

June

June Hunt

WORRY
The Joy Stealer

Jesus says *don't* … but we do it anyway.

And because we do, we become tense and troubled. Multiple times Jesus says clearly, specifically, unequivocally, *"Do not worry about your life"* (Matthew 6:25)—meaning, do not worry about *anything* in your life.

Not anything? Is that even possible?

When we worry, we allow our irreplaceable time to waste away. Worrying about the length of your life will not add one day to your life. Spending an entire night stressing over a problem won't usher in a solution any more than an afternoon of fretting over your finances will fix them.

For some, worry seems as natural as blinking. Many assume that being worry-free is merely wishful thinking. That is, until we experience firsthand just how personal God is and how faithful He is to meet our deepest inner needs.

Jesus reasons with us: If God faithfully provides food for the birds, won't He much more provide for you—especially since you have far more value?

Knowing just how much worry *wears* you down, Jesus lovingly reminds you …

"Do not worry."
Luke 12:22

DEFINITIONS

You've seen them. You've met them. You know them. Maybe you are one of them: the worriers.

Worriers don't fully relax. They don't let their guard down. At night, they toss and turn, regretting today and dreading tomorrow. Worriers are convinced that around every corner calamity lurks just waiting to pounce.

Worriers fear they won't have sufficient funds *for the future.* Or they won't meet someone else's expectations *ever!* They fret about what people *will think*—or worse—what people *will say*, especially about them. And if they aren't worrying about something, they agonize over the thought that they have somehow missed something to worry about!

Like a merry-go-round in an outdoor playground, 'round and 'round and 'round they go in a tiring attempt to control everything in their lives. Yet the truth remains: Worrying will never make you "merry," nor can it enhance your present life or even prepare you for the future.

Jesus pinpoints this truth ...

> "Can all your worries add
> a single moment to your life?
> ... Don't worry about tomorrow,
> for tomorrow will bring its own worries.
> Today's trouble is enough for today."
> Matthew 6:27, 34 NLT

Whether you find yourself in a frustrating situation, or facing an unknown future, worrying can seem so normal, so typical, so logical. However, you need to ask yourself two simple, but sensible, questions: "How has worrying helped me in the past?" And, "How will worrying help me in the future?" Our master teacher Jesus makes His point clear ...

> "So do not worry, saying,
> 'What shall we eat?' or 'What shall
> we drink?' or 'What shall we wear?'"
> Matthew 6:31

Worrying is useless, pointless, worthless. And more so, to live in a constant state of angst is absolutely exhausting. So what do you need to know about worry?

▶ **Worry** is *mental distress*[1] primarily over a negative possibility in the future.

- Worry is a state of mind, a way of thinking, a mental habit.[2]

- Worry is a preoccupation with something bad that may happen, may not happen, or cannot happen.

"My thoughts trouble me and I am distraught" (Psalm 55:2).

▶ **Worry** in English is derived from the Old German word *wurgen*, meaning "to strangle or choke."[3]

- Worry is a thief that steals joy and strangles faith.

- Worry is a destroyer when it chokes the Word of God from us, keeping our lives from bearing fruit.

Jesus says, *"The worries of this life … come in and choke the word, making it unfruitful"* (Mark 4:19).

▶ **Worry** divides the mind between what is motivating and demotivating, what is constructive and destructive.

- Worry in the New Testament is the Greek word, *merimnao*, meaning to worry anxiously, to be distracted by—literally to have a divided mind.[4]

- The Greek word *merimnao* comes from two words: *merizo*, "to draw in different directions, to divide"[5] and *nous*, "the mind."[6]

The worrier can be compared to *"a person … double-minded and unstable in all they do"* (James 1:8).

The Brain and Worry Systems

QUESTION: "How does worry impact the brain?"

ANSWER: Your body has been created by God with a physical defense system that is ready to be activated when you are in danger. Consider how this defense system works within your brain.

▶ **Excessive worry** causes a distress signal to be sent to the brain's "command center" (the hypothalamus).

- The "traffic cop" portion of the brain (the amygdala), in concert with the brain's command center (hypothalamus) directs the "taxi cabs"

11

(carrying adrenaline and cortisol) to bypass the thinking center (the cortex) and instead to go straight to the emotional center (the limbic system).

- The reward/pleasure center (the nucleus accumbens) welcomes the "feel good" chemical (dopamine) and creates a growing desire for more even though the situation causing the worry is not necessarily a healthy or positive source.

▶ **Excessive worry** activates the physical defense system quickly, before the brain's visual centers can fully process what is happening.

- The brain is basically saying, "Don't think about what's happening—just feel it and react to it."

- The more often this process occurs, the more easily traveled the brain's superhighway (neural pathway in the brain) becomes where adrenaline and dopamine create an unhealthy craving for more of the same. Over time, this well-worn pathway can become a rut. It takes greater effort to get out of a rut than it does to steer around one.

"You will keep in perfect peace
those whose minds are steadfast,
because they trust in you."
Isaiah 26:3

Where is your focus? Is it on your future—the unknown events in your life yet to occur? Is it on your past—on the frequently rehearsed painful events that have shaped your life? Or is it on your faithful God—how He has been your sufficiency in the past, and how He will be your provider in the future?

You can replace your fretful worry with faith. Jesus illustrates this by asking you to observe how God's caregiving extends even to clothing grassy fields with wildflowers.

> "Consider how the wild flowers grow.
> They do not labor or spin.
> Yet I tell you, not even Solomon in all
> his splendor was dressed like one of these.
> If that is how God clothes the grass
> of the field, which is here today,
> and tomorrow is thrown into the fire,
> how much more will he clothe you—
> you of little faith!"
> Luke 12:27–28

The Wearying "What-Ifs" of Worry

It's been said that life is a "meteor shower of what-ifs."[7] If you are a worrier, you likely spend a great deal of time wondering about the "what-ifs"—what may or may not happen. Then, worrying about the worst, you get caught up in speculating.

▶ **"What if** I don't finish in time?"

▶ **"What if** I lose my job? My savings?"

▶ **"What if** I don't have enough money?"

▶ **"What if** I fail?"

▶ **"What if** I don't know what to do?"

▶ **"What if** I can't meet expectations?"

▶ **"What if** I have a really bad experience?"

▶ **"What if** I don't have enough time?"

▶ **"What if** I get too stressed out?"

▶ **"What if** I make a mistake or do it wrong?"

▶ **"What if** I make a fool of myself?"

▶ **"What if** I never meet my soulmate?"

▶ **"What if** someone I love is hurt?"

▶ **"What if** I am rejected?"

▶ **"What if** I become seriously ill?"

▶ **"What if** I can't take care of myself?"

▶ **"What if** I end up all alone?"

▶ **"What if** I run out of options?"

These speculative, often fatalistic, "what-ifs" can paralyze your present and obscure your future. Your mind cannot be consumed with worry about future possibilities and solve present-day problems at the same time.

Instead of worrying about the negative "what-ifs," you can make a conscious decision not to be distracted, distressed, or distraught with worry. *What if* instead, you put your trust in God and placed your confidence in Him?

> "Whoever dwells in the shelter of the Most
> High will rest in the shadow of the Almighty.
> I will say of the LORD,
> 'He is my refuge and my fortress,
> my God, in whom I trust.'"
> Psalm 91:1–2

Fear vs. Worry

QUESTION: **"What is the difference between fear and worry?"**

ANSWER: Fear is an *emotional* reaction to a perceived, *present* danger. Whereas worry is *mental distress* over a possible, undesired happening in the *future*.

▶ **Fear** focuses on present events and is energizing when it propels a person to action in a way that removes or lessens real danger.

▶ **Worry** is distracting and can lead to distress, despair, and even depression and anxiety. In addition, worry is unproductive because it projects problems and unknown future events.

Fear sees a threat. Worry imagines one.[8]

The Lord offers these comforting words to those overwhelmed with worry ...

> "Call on me in the day of trouble;
> I will deliver you, and you will honor me."
> Psalm 50:15

QUESTION: "How do I know if I'm dealing with worry or anxiety?"

ANSWER: People often use the words *worry* and *anxiety* interchangeably. However, there are key differences between the two.

▶ **Worry** is typically understood to be a *mental* process—ruminating on "what-if" scenarios that may or may not come to fruition in the future. It is often anticipating an outcome, attempting to solve a problem, or avoiding a deeper issue. Worry is not an emotion or a feeling—like joy, anger, or love. However, worry can reveal a hidden fear. Worry is not an emotion, but it can lead to feeling anxious.

▶ **Anxiety** is a present physiological feeling, usually an emotional response to a current or possible future threat (real or perceived). Anxiety becomes problematic when it is excessive or persistent (with individual episodes extending six months or more) known as Generalized Anxiety Disorder (GAD).[9] Excessive, obsessive worry can lead to anxiety. Likewise, stress can lead to worry or anxiety. Anxiety can also make an appearance all on its own.

Stress vs. Worry

QUESTION: "What is the relationship between stress and worry?"

ANSWER: Stress and worry are closely related, but they are not the same.

▶ **Stress** is a natural response to a challenge. It is normal and, to some extent, a necessary part of life. Stress can be triggered by an event that makes you feel nervous, angry, or frustrated. But not all stress is bad. There's a good stress, too. For a student, the moderate stress of an exam typically provides motivation to study. Likewise, with no homework to turn in and no regular tests to take, many students would be unmotivated to study.

▶ **Worry** is a reaction to stress. If a student thinks he or she can't handle a particular challenge (such as giving a speech in class), it adds pressure and he or she begins to feel out of control and, ultimately, becomes worried and afraid. Worry is like being caught in a spiral—stressful elements churn around and around in your mind making it very difficult, if not impossible, to sort out.

Stress and worry share many of the same physical symptoms: fatigue, muscle tension, increased heartbeat, mood swings, difficulty concentrating or making decisions, a change in appetite, and trouble sleeping.

With stress, you generally know what you're dealing with—a looming deadline, bills, a relationship issue. Whereas with worry you're less likely to be aware of what you're actually anxious about and, thus, your reaction becomes the problem.

Stress and worry can both lead to *unrest*. And the enemy wants to use the *unrest* to *arrest* you—to hold you captive to the worries and stresses of life. But God's plan—His path for both stress and worry—leads not to painful unrest, but rather to peaceful rest. The enemy wants to overwhelm you with unrest, but the Lord wants you to overcome with His rest. If you want to find peace in times of stress or worry, come to the Lord and find the rest you're looking for in Him.

> "Let me teach you, because
> I am humble and gentle at heart,
> and you will find rest for your souls."
> Matthew 11:29 NLT

WHAT IS Concern?

Carrie discovers the company she's working for is downsizing and her job is being eliminated. Her manager feels terrible, as does Carrie, a single mom with two elementary-age children. Without an income, her family problems loom large.

However, instead of worrying about what *might* happen if she fails to find employment, Carrie immediately jumps into action. She updates her resume, and looks and applies for jobs. She watches job boards and networks with family, friends, and former coworkers. She stays active and positive while looking for a new job. Carrie expresses appropriate concern over losing her job, which spurs her to action as she manages the consequences of her job loss.

Concern lives in the moment without ignoring the realities of life. Concern sees problems and challenges for what they are, yet keeps moving forward. *Worry*, on the other hand, sees the problems and challenges but gets stuck in them. Therefore, forward momentum stutters and stalls.

This means you can decide: Will you stay stuck in the web of worry or will you move forward with confident concern, knowing God has a wonderful plan for your life that will be sovereignly fulfilled as you trust in Him?

> "Trust in the LORD with all your heart
> and lean not on your own understanding;
> in all your ways submit to him,
> and he will make your paths straight."
> Proverbs 3:5–6

▶ **Concern** engages your attention, interest, and care, and even affects your sense of well-being.[10]

▶ **Concern** comes from the late fifteenth century medieval Latin word *concernere*, meaning "to affect the interest of, be of importance to."[11]

▶ **Concern** demonstrates your personal maturity and growth. When you have concern, you have the ability to see reality, feel empathy and compassion, and care about others.[12]

▶ **Concern** propels you to act constructively—such as seeing a doctor when you are ill or getting help from a mechanic when your car makes strange sounds. Active concern is productive.

Like David, we can implore God …

> "Guide me in your truth and teach me,
> for you are God my Savior,
> and my hope is in you all day long."
> Psalm 25:5

The spectrum of concern can range from careless apathy to appropriate concern. But beyond concern lies the woes of worry and anxiety—from mild or moderate to severe and severely debilitating. Depending on the degree, worry can seem somewhat manageable or reach a level so severe it interferes with daily life and makes living a moment-to-moment struggle.

People experiencing only a small measure of worry might ignore feelings of apprehension or even avoid situations that make them uncomfortable. Others who experience a stronger sense of worry that leads to anxiety might address the situation causing the angst, yet resent being in that position and fear dealing with a similar situation in the future.[13]

We must turn our focus from our fears to the Lord who is with us in the midst of our distress. We can then say with assurance …

"Though I walk in the midst of trouble,
you preserve my life."
Psalm 138:7

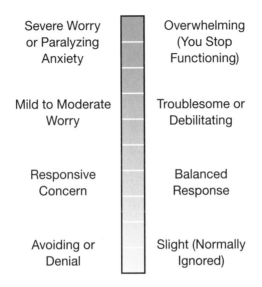

Severe Worry or Paralyzing Anxiety	Overwhelming (You Stop Functioning)
Mild to Moderate Worry	Troublesome or Debilitating
Responsive Concern	Balanced Response
Avoiding or Denial	Slight (Normally Ignored)

Most people experience some times of periodic worry, but not everyone experiences worry in the same way or to the same degree. We need to recognize when concern increases to worry and use it as a motivation to trust in the Lord all the more.

To the troubled heart, Jesus says …

> "Do not let your hearts be troubled.
> You believe in God; believe also in me."
> John 14:1

▶ **Mild to Moderate Worry**

Normal fear generates concern, but slips into worry when ...

- It becomes repetitive.

- It becomes extensive and pervasive.

- It potentially motivates, but often undermines momentum.

- It prevents you from fully trusting, living dependently on the Lord.

Notice that the psalmist, who put these words to music, turned his focus to the Lord when feeling distraught ...

"When I worried about many things,
your assuring words soothed my soul."
Psalm 94:19 GW

▶ **Severe Worry**

Severe worry is when you become emotionally stuck and are unable to cope with a past or present problem. It inhibits you from moving forward into the future with confidence.[14] Severe worry—abnormal, fearful obsession—is more profound and problematic when ...

- It makes concentration difficult.

- It causes forgetfulness.

- It hinders normal functioning.

- It blocks communication with others.

Notice that Solomon, known as the wisest man on earth, said …

> "Banish anxiety from your heart."
> Ecclesiastes 11:10

WHAT ARE Four Characterizations of the Spectrum of Concern?

Imagine four siblings. They have grown up in the same home, gone to the same schools, and have been raised by the same parents. They all work together for the same family business and all encounter the same crisis: their father (who runs the family business) has been diagnosed with cancer. But observe how their thinking differs as they share the same stresses and strains.

Each of the four needs to remember …

> "The LORD is good,
> a refuge in times of trouble.
> He cares for those who trust in him."
> Nahum 1:7

▶ **Carefree Connie** generally seems worry-free and stress-free but often comes across as uncaring and irresponsible. Connie thinks:

- "I live by '*don't worry, be happy.*'"

- "This isn't my problem."

- "Why worry? It'll work out somehow."

- "Yes, I've said I care, but I need to do what I think is best for me."

"Since God has allowed us to be happy, we will not worry too much about how short life is" (Ecclesiastes 5:20 GNT).

▶ **Controlling Travis** seeks stability when he feels out of control. Travis thinks:

- "I have to take control."

- "If I don't take care of this, no one will."

- "If I don't handle this, everything will go wrong."

- "I can't let this happen. Everyone depends on me."

"'You will not succeed by your own strength or by your own power, but by my Spirit,' says the LORD All-Powerful" (Zechariah 4:6 NCV).

▶ **Consumed Susan** is paralyzed by constant worry. Susan thinks:

- "I can't help but worry all the time."

- "This is going to be bad. I know it won't end well."

- "Why does this always happen to me?"

- "There's no way out. I can't do anything but worry."

"You work and worry your way through life, and what do you have to show for it?" (Ecclesiastes 2:22 GNT).

▶ **Concerned Chris** handles worry in a planned and intentional way; it moves him to appropriate action. Chris thinks:

- "I will entrust my life to the Lord to take care of me and what concerns me."

- "God doesn't want me consumed with worry, so I'm praying and seeking His guidance."

- "Instead of worrying, I'm going to seek wise counsel and experienced advice."

- "I'm concerned about you, so I want to know how you're doing and how I can help."

"Be careful to do what the LORD your God has commanded you; do not turn aside to the right or to the left" (Deuteronomy 5:32).

Sin or Not?

QUESTION: "Is worry a sin?"

ANSWER: Yes, Scripture clearly shows that worry runs contrary to God's plan for us.[15]

- **Worry** is not just a problem of the mind (mental), it is also a problem of the heart (spiritual) because it involves relying on someone or something rather than on God.

- **Worry** gets in the way of faith and reveals a lack of trust in God.

- **Worry** can take on a life of its own and become an "enemy within," distracting you with its relentless flow of bothersome thoughts.

- **Worry** fools you into thinking that it is directed at solving problems, but it never delivers a solution.

- **Worry** is a failure to trust God, thus we need God's grace and truth when we worry.

You may feel that you'll never be able to overcome the habit of worrying. But nothing is too hard for God. Realize, Jesus died for you on the cross and rose again. In doing so, He overcame death. Therefore, He can help you conquer your worrisome thoughts. Next time worry pays you a visit, don't answer the door. Instead, choose to set your mind on the myriad of ways God has seen you through actual difficulties (not imagined ones), and let your heart be filled with gratitude for all the times He's protected and provided for you.

> "I will praise you, Lord, with all my heart;
> I will tell of all the marvelous things
> you have done."
> Psalm 9:1 NLT

WHAT IS God's Heart on Worry?

When we worry, our minds get an unnecessary workout. We run through all the possible outcomes to our situation. We jump to conclusions before getting all the facts. We weigh ourselves down with all the "what-ifs."

Truly, worrying is an exercise in futility. Worry leads to fear and stress instead of faith and rest.

Realize, when Jesus talked about worry, He redirected our focus onto God. He wants us to understand that our worries don't change the character of God. Ultimately, grasping God's character changes how we handle our worries. Perhaps the most poignant phrase Jesus said to worriers is "*your heavenly Father knows*" (Matthew 6:32).

God knows what's going on in your life. He cares about what's happening. He loves you. While worry will steal your joy, the Lord gives it. He wants every worried heart to look to Him for help and find joy.

"I prayed to the Lord, and he answered me.
He freed me from all my fears.
Those who look to him for help
will be radiant with joy."
Psalm 34:4–5 NLT

▶ **God wants** you to remember that He is good and gracious and cares about you with compassion.

"The Lord is gracious and compassionate, slow to anger and rich in love. The Lord is good to all; he has compassion on all he has made" (Psalm 145:8–9).

▶ **God wants** you to remember that He promises to meet your needs.

"The Lord will guide you always; he will satisfy your needs in a sun-scorched land and will strengthen your frame" (Isaiah 58:11).

▶ **God wants** you not to live in a state of worry.

"Do not worry about tomorrow, for tomorrow will worry about itself. Each day has enough trouble of its own" (Matthew 6:34).

▶ **God wants** you to trust Him when you're worried— to have faith and not fear.

"When I am afraid, I put my trust in you" (Psalm 56:3).

▶ **God wants** to be close to you when worries break your heart.

"The LORD is close to the brokenhearted; he rescues those whose spirits are crushed" (Psalm 34:18 NLT).

▶ **God wants** you to look to Him when you're filled with worry.

"When anxiety was great within me, your consolation brought me joy" (Psalm 94:19).

▶ **God wants** you to look to His Word when you're tempted to worry.

"As pressure and stress bear down on me, I find joy in your commands" (Psalm 119:143 NLT).

▶ **God wants** you to give Him all your worries because He cares for you.

"Give all your worries and cares to God, for he cares about you" (1 Peter 5:7 NLT).

▶ **God wants** you to encourage others when they are worried.

"Encourage one another and build each other up" (1 Thessalonians 5:11).

▶ **God wants** you to talk with Him about everything that's worrying you, and thank Him for how He will use the trials in your life.

"Don't worry about anything; instead, pray about everything. Tell God what you need, and thank him for all he has done. Then you will experience God's peace, which exceeds anything we can understand. His peace will guard your hearts and minds as you live in Christ Jesus" (Philippians 4:6–7 NLT).

CHARACTERISTICS

Whether it's politics, popularity, or performance, people feel insecure under the weight of all their worry. If only they understood the love the Lord has for them, they could rest from their worries.

> "Let the beloved of the LORD rest secure
> in him, for he shields him all day long,
> and the one the LORD loves rests
> between his shoulders."
> Deuteronomy 33:12

WHAT Characterizes Common Webs of Worry?

Worry can work its way into your life like an unwanted visitor. This intruder will fill your mind with endless echoes of *"what if … what if … what if?"* Worry weaves webs that trap and tangle up your thoughts. It steals your sleep, stifles your joy, and preys on your peace.

The Bible recounts David's plea followed by his acknowledgment of God's provision ...

> "Give me relief from my distress;
> have mercy on me and hear my prayer. …
> Fill my heart with joy …
> In peace I will lie down and sleep,
> for you alone, LORD, make me dwell in safety."
> Psalm 4:1, 7–8

Webs of Worry

Place a check mark (✔) beside the statements that are true of you.

12 MENTAL Webs of Worry

❑ I consistently worry over disappointing others.

❑ I fret over my future.

❑ I obsess over the possibility of bad news.

❑ I struggle to enjoy life, assuming something will go wrong.

❑ I become distraught when unjust people succeed.

❑ I become stressed out by thoughts of making a mistake.

❑ I obsess over thoughts of death or dying.

❑ I become preoccupied over every little thing.

❑ I become frequently distracted by worry.

❑ I become hyperalert, constantly contemplating danger.

❑ I have difficulty concentrating.

❑ I have difficulty remembering.

12 PHYSICAL Webs of Worry

❑ I have difficulty sleeping.

❑ I have an increased or decreased appetite.

❑ I have muscle tension or backaches.

❑ I have a rapid heartbeat or dizziness.

- ❏ I experience shortness of breath.
- ❏ I find it hard to relax.
- ❏ I perspire excessively.
- ❏ I experience nausea or stomach discomfort.
- ❏ I often sigh heavily.
- ❏ I have changes in my blood pressure or blood sugar.
- ❏ I have frequent headaches.
- ❏ I experience increased fatigue.

12 BEHAVIORAL Webs of Worry

- ❏ I find myself being unusually fidgety.
- ❏ I engage in foot tapping or nail biting.
- ❏ I find myself being irritable.
- ❏ I act jumpy and on edge.
- ❏ I think I am overly talkative.
- ❏ I notice my voice quivering.
- ❏ I often find myself staring into space.
- ❏ I escape through alcohol, pornography, or other addictions.
- ❏ I frequently blame others for my actions or behaviors.
- ❏ I experience body trembling or twitching unexpectedly.
- ❏ I slip back into childish ways of coping.
- ❏ I find it difficult to make decisions.

12 SPIRITUAL Webs of Worry

❑ I worry about my spiritual destiny.

❑ I fear being judged by God.

❑ I worry about my salvation.

❑ I think I'm not doing enough for God.

❑ I question the goodness of God.

❑ I obsess over what will happen after I die.

❑ I have a reduced desire to pray or read Scripture.

❑ I feel bitter toward God when He seems silent.

❑ I have a diminished interest in church and other Christian gatherings.

❑ I blame God for letting bad things happen.

❑ I believe I need to be perfect to protect my salvation.

❑ I put my faith primarily in myself instead of God.

If you selected any of these statements, listen to the words of Jesus ...

"Come to me, all you who are weary and
burdened, and I will give you rest.
Take my yoke upon you and learn from me,
for I am gentle and humble in heart,
and you will find rest for your souls.
For my yoke is easy and my burden is light."
Matthew 11:28–30

Let's return to our example of four siblings—Connie, Travis, Susan, and Chris—who are dealing with the aftermath of their father's cancer diagnosis. Dad is sick and Mom is focused on caregiving. The four brothers and sisters are dealing with the emotional upheaval of their father's illness and also struggling with an additional issue—a downturn in the family business. Dad built the business and much of its reputation rests on his involvement. His children now have the responsibility of providing for their employees, suppliers, and their individual families. So when facing possible layoffs to keep the business afloat, how do each of the siblings respond?

"Cast your cares on the LORD
and he will sustain you;
he will never let the righteous be shaken."
Psalm 55:22

▶ **Carefree Connie**

- Feels on a typically shallow level: "I don't really care what happens. I can't do anything about it."

- Feelings come across as apathetic: "If you want to worry, that's your problem."

- Appears uncaring and unconcerned: "I couldn't care less."

- Denies worrying: "I never worry about anything."

- Avoids responsibilities: "It's not my job to worry."

- Remains silent about concerns: "What worry?"

"'Which of these three do you think was a neighbor to the man who fell into the hands of robbers?' The expert in the law replied, 'The one who had mercy on him.' Jesus told him, 'Go and do likewise'" (Luke 10:36–37).

▶ Controlling Travis

- Feels out of control: "If I'm not in charge, I feel out of control."

- Feels insecure: "I'm afraid of what will happen if I don't take charge."

- Fears losing control and may internalize worry: "If I don't know what's going on, I worry about what will happen."

- Worry leads to excessive work and busyness: "The only way I don't worry about something getting done is to oversee everything myself."

- Rationalizes behavior as planning for possible outcomes: "I'm not worrying. I'm taking care of issues before they can become problems."

- Plans or analyzes and remains hypervigilant: "I'm always watching to analyze every situation, think through every possible result, and try to plan ahead what I might do or what I want someone else to do."

Jesus said, *"Martha, Martha ... you are worried and upset about many things"* (Luke 10:41).

▶ Consumed Susan

- Feels irritable or depressed: "Worrying takes up so much energy. I feel angry, exhausted, and depressed."

- Feels helpless and has a victim mentality: "If anything bad is going to happen, it will always happen to me."

- Paralyzed by worry and feels stuck: "I worry all the time. I don't know what to do, which makes me worry even more."

- Imagination runs wild with possible outcomes, worst-case scenarios, and disproportionately catastrophic thinking that develops into panic: "When I hear about terrible things happening, I'm sure it will happen to me or someone I love."

- Lacks sleep, develops depression, and has a negative outlook: "I can't stop worrying, so I don't sleep. I'm left feeling depressed and I don't have any hope."

- Vents about worries constantly or experiences intense internalization: "When I try to talk to people about my worries, they don't want to listen. No one cares about me anymore."

"We were under great pressure, far beyond our ability to endure, so that we despaired of life itself" (2 Corinthians 1:8).

▶ **Concerned Chris**

- Feels appropriate care and concern: "This situation concerns me."

- Sensitive and perceptive, and is aware of the needs of others: "I can see that my loved ones are struggling with a problem."

- Prays regularly: "Before I do anything else, I'm going to pray."

- Remembers and rests in God's promises: "I'm not going to worry because I know God is in control."

- Takes proactive steps about legitimate concerns: "Based on what I read in the Bible, I know God would want me to do what I can to help."

- Reaches out to others to offer help when concerned: "I will offer to come alongside my family and friends during this difficult time."

"We are hard pressed on every side, but not crushed; perplexed, but not in despair" (2 Corinthians 4:8).

WHAT Differentiates Destructive Worry from Constructive Concern?

Sometimes only a fine line seems to separate worry and concern. But these close cousins are polar opposites in terms of the results each brings. There is a world of difference between *destructive worry* and *constructive concern*.

Worry divides your mind and prevents productivity. Concern, on the other hand, is a legitimate response to situations that signal danger or call us to preventative action. But be careful—*unchecked concern* can quickly turn into a runaway worry train! Faith is needed to "put on the brakes"—faith in the Lord that He will provide what He promises: food to eat, water to drink, and clothes to wear.

Jesus assures us …

"Your Father knows that you need them."
Luke 12:30

Destructive Worry vs. Constructive Concern[16]

DESTRUCTIVE WORRY	CONSTRUCTIVE CONCERN
Promotes inaction	Prompts action
Disrupts a plan	Puts a plan together
Feels out of control	Takes control where possible
Ignores or blocks reality	Demonstrates the ability to see reality
Distracts from the problem	Focuses on the problem
Shows self-absorbed, selfish tendencies	Feels empathy or compassion
Is destructive, unhealthy, misplaced	Is constructive, healthy, focused
Remains immature; stunts growth	Produces maturity and growth

When we defend our tendency to worry as being only genuine concern, honest reflection requires that we take a close look at our hearts and minds.[17]

EXAMPLE:

▶ **Destructive worry:** "I'm so worried my child might drown. I'll never let her near any body of water. That way I can keep her safe."

▶ **Constructive concern:** "I'm so concerned my child might drown. I've made arrangements for her to take swimming lessons so I can help her be safe."

DESTRUCTIVE WORRY	CONSTRUCTIVE CONCERN
Paralyzes	Mobilizes
Decreases creativity	Increases creativity
Prevents initiative	Promotes initiative
Results in anxious fretting	Results in calm focusing
Attempts to control the future	Attempts to improve the future
Fears the worst	Hopes for the best
Appears negative to others	Appears positive to others
Distracts the mind from what is important	Directs the mind to what is important

If you find your initial *concern* has turned into consuming worry, change your perspective, turn from a temporal focus on things of this world to an eternal focus on what God values in heaven. As Colossians 3:2 says, *"Set your minds on things above, not on earthly things."* And when you find yourself being concerned about a situation or circumstance you do not know how to handle, remember that you can act on this promise ...

> "If any of you lacks wisdom,
> you should ask God,
> who gives generously to all without finding
> fault, and it will be given to you."
> James 1:5

Worried Christian

QUESTION: "I worry all the time. Does this mean I'm not a good Christian?"

ANSWER: God doesn't qualify or quantify your status as a Christian. While it's true that God wants you to continue to build and develop trust in Him, He remains patient and faithful to walk with you through the ups and downs of your life.

You may experience anxiety at the thought of speaking in public, or face an irrational fear of snow even if you live in a desert. You may not have the boldness of Daniel facing the lions' den or his three friends entering the fiery furnace. But know this: Whatever God calls you to do, He will equip you to do it. The Bible says, *"The one who calls you is faithful, and he will do it"* (1 Thessalonians 5:24).

God's Word tells us that even Jesus was *"deeply distressed and troubled … overwhelmed with sorrow"* as He was praying in the garden of Gethsemane before His arrest and betrayal leading to His death on the cross.

Feeling anxious or struggling with worry doesn't make you an inferior Christian. It simply means you are human.[18] Still, God loves you and wants you to live the best life possible, which involves depending on Him for provision, seeking His will, following His instructions, and trusting His character and faithfulness. Remember this truth about God …

> **"For great is your love,**
> **reaching to the heavens;**
> **your faithfulness reaches to the skies."**
> **Psalm 57:10**

WHAT IS the "What-If" Cycle of Worry?

When Jesus speaks from a boat on the lake to the crowds gathered around Him, He tells a parable. Today, some recognize the story in Matthew 13 as the "Parable of the Seeds," but it's actually known as the "Parable of the Sower." The seeds are incidental to the story. *Where* the seeds are sown by the sower is the central message of the story.

A farmer scatters seed and some falls along the path, but birds eat the seed. Some seed falls into rocky soil where shoots come up, but are scorched by the sun in the shallow soil. Some seed falls among the thorns, which eventually chokes the very life from the plants. But some seed falls on good soil, which yields a bountiful crop.

Jesus explains the meaning within the parable: His message about the kingdom of God is sown in the world.

▶ When people don't understand, the enemy of their souls snatches away what is sown in their hearts like the birds snatching seed along the path.

▶ The seed on rocky ground represents those who hear the Word of God and immediately accept it with joy. But with no sustaining roots, it lasts only a short while before trouble takes its toll.

▶ The seed on good soil refers to those who hear God's Word and understand it.

▶ Finally, the seed among the thorns represents the Word choked by the worries of life.

> "The worries of this life …
> choke the word, making it unfruitful."
> Matthew 13:22

The Worry Cycle[19]

Realize, the cycle of worry is a downward spiral, spinning in circles until anything good is strangled by the choking grasp of "what-ifs." A fragment of fear starts the cycle of worry.

EXAMPLE:

Imagine, your family plans a trip to the beach. You hear on the news that a shark has been sighted near your destination. Soon, the worry cycle starts.

▶ If a shark has been sighted, there must be more than one.

▶ And if there's more than one shark, the odds are we will see one while we're at the beach.

▶ But if we don't see a shark, how many more are there that we cannot see?

▶ And if there are sharks we cannot see, then we can't be safe in the water.

▶ And if we're not safe in the water, we'll get too hot on the sand.

▶ And if we're too hot on the sand, we could suffer a heatstroke.

▶ And if we could suffer a heatstroke on the beach, we should probably just stay in our room.

▶ So if we're going to stay in our room, what's the point of going to the beach? Maybe we should just stay home! Then we don't have to worry about a plane crash, a car wreck, losing our luggage, our identities being stolen, getting food poisoning … and especially not being eaten by a shark!

The answer to stopping the "what-if" cycle of worry is to refuse to get on that not-so-merry-go-round in the first place. When you trust God, He invites you to trust Him with everything.

"Those who know your name trust in you,
for you, LORD, have never forsaken
those who seek you."
Psalm 9:10

CAUSES

The meaning for "worry wart" might relate to the long-held belief (a myth) that warts are caused by worry and, consequently, the term is currently used as a metaphor for someone who worries incessantly.

However, the words of Jesus should be taken literally as a deterrent to worry …

> "Can any one of you by worrying add
> a single hour to your life?"
> Matthew 6:27

WHAT ARE the Core Causes of Worry?

Do you catch yourself worrying over things you cannot control, and wonder *why* you worry?

Think back to when Jesus appeared before His disciples by walking on water toward their boat (Matthew 14:22–33). Peter asked Jesus to summon him, and Jesus said to Peter, *"Come"* (Matthew 14:29). Miraculously, Peter began walking on the water. But when he took his eyes off Jesus, he looked down, became afraid, and then began to sink. Peter cried out, *"Lord, save me!"*

> "Immediately Jesus reached out his hand
> and caught him. 'You of little faith,'
> he said, 'why did you doubt?'"
> Matthew 14:31

From the Lord's perspective—since Jesus says, *"Don't worry"*—you need to see worry as a choice: either worry or live by faith in Him. Faith means taking God at His word and totally trusting what He says.

The Two Core Causes of Worry

1. **Disbelief**—You choose not to believe what Jesus literally says. You really *don't believe* God when He says He will provide all that you need.

   "Despite all the miraculous signs Jesus had done, most of the people still did not believe in him" (John 12:37 NLT).

   Even when followers walked and talked with Jesus who performed miracle after miracle, most of the onlookers still did not take Him at face value. They did not believe that what Jesus told them about Himself was the absolute truth. When we worry, are we not doing the same?

2. **Disobedience**—You choose not to obey what Jesus literally says. You are choosing to be *disobedient* when you worry about what God has promised to provide.

   Jesus says, *"I tell you, do not worry about your life, what you will eat or drink; or about your body, what you will wear. Is not life more than food, and the body more than clothes?"* (Matthew 6:25).

   Jesus isn't making a mere suggestion—He's stating a command. When God commands us to do something and we refuse, we are choosing to disobey Him. This disobedience is a sin.

1. **Belief**—Choose to believe what Jesus literally says. Stop doubting and believe that God will meet all your needs (not all your "wants," but all your needs).

   "[Jesus] said to Thomas, 'Put your finger here; see my hands. Reach out your hand and put it into my side. Stop doubting and believe'" (John 20:27).

   We, like doubting Thomas, would do well to stop doubting. God *will* provide, God *will* protect, God *will* prove faithful in our lives.

2. **Obedience**—Choose to obey what Jesus literally says. Stop struggling with worry and allow the Lord to meet your needs.

   "The LORD will guide you always; he will satisfy your needs in a sun-scorched land and will strengthen your frame. You will be like a well-watered garden, like a spring whose waters never fail" (Isaiah 58:11).

   Obedience and faith go hand in hand. The best way to build faith and grow in obedience is by reading the Word of God and letting it read you (let the Bible show you where you need to change). As you begin to read and personalize Scripture, your faith in God will increase and your worry will begin to decrease.

As we try to make sense of our emotional tensions (our worries), we are tempted to look "out there" to identify things happening around us that create and perpetuate worry.

The tensions and worries we often experience are *not* due to a hostile environment, but rather to our own misguided choices.

> "Don't you realize that you become the slave of whatever you choose to obey? You can be a slave to sin, which leads to death, or you can choose to obey God, which leads to righteous living."
> **Romans 6:16** NLT

For instance, do you …

▶ **Believe** life would be virtually stress-free if there was only more money in the bank, even though limited income is not necessarily what causes cash flow problems?

▶ **Find yourself** committing to too many activities, overloading your schedule, and complicating your life and the lives of those around you?

▶ **Go too far** in serving your kids' needs—to the extent that you inadvertently teach them to be self-indulgent and disrespectful of your needs and limitations as a parent?

▶ **Fail to take care** of your own physical needs by not getting adequate sleep, not eating balanced meals, not exercising regularly, and not balancing busyness and rest?

▶ **Allow your life** to be dominated by people who are not good for you—people who exert a negative influence, drain your emotional energy, or stir up conflict?

▶ **Tend to put off** responsibilities you find difficult or unpleasant to the point that they cause unwanted repercussions?

Letting go of worry begins by examining your own life honestly and openly before the Lord.

> "Test me, Lord, and try me,
> examine my heart and my mind."
> Psalm 26:2

WHAT Other Factors Contribute to Worry?

Are any of these statements true about you?

- "Sometimes I lie awake at night worrying about something that happened during the day."

- "When I make a mistake at work, I am far more concerned about it than my coworkers are."

- "Going to the doctor always makes me uneasy because of what the exam might reveal."

If your answer is *yes*, take to heart the following scripture ...

> "You will keep in perfect peace those
> whose minds are steadfast,
> because they trust in you."
> Isaiah 26:3

Throughout the day, there are many opportunities to worry. But have you ever stopped to think about what prompts you to worry? Besides trials (specific to you), life (as a whole), and daily news reports (from around the world), several other factors contribute to worry. These include:[20]

▶ **Biology/Genetics**—These worriers could be "wired" to worry.

- Some people are born with a predisposition to anxiety (worry is often tied to anxiety). They have a genetic makeup (related to encoded personality traits) that brings out the worrier in them.

- In 2007, Yale researchers identified a gene variation associated with chronic worrying. The "worry gene" as it's called, is the result of a genetic mutation that predicts a person's tendency to "overthink" or obsess over negative thoughts.[21]

- Areas of the brain are linked along a circuit. The way the brain is wired regulates how someone responds to danger or threats. In some, more than the norm, this circuitry is more activated causing more anxiety and frustration.[22]

▶ **Life Circumstances**—These worriers have learned over time how to worry in response to their unpredictable, powerless environments.

- Difficult life experiences can bring worry to our lives. They make us more aware of how uncertain everyday life is and shake our confidence. (Example: Living through a natural disaster or an economic crash can leave you waiting for the "other shoe to drop.")

- Negative life experiences increase our feelings of vulnerability and powerlessness. The more we experience these feelings and don't know what to do with them, the easier it is to worry. (Example: You grew up in an alcoholic or violent family where unpredictability was the norm, so you remain hypervigilant and alert for the possibility of trouble.)

- Worry is a way to feel in control or avoid the reality of a present situation that feels unstable. Out-of-control situations often trigger worry.

▶ **Traumatic Experiences**—These worriers experienced unresolved trauma which can trigger unrelenting worry.

- Loss that is unexpected, traumatic, or difficult can lead to future worry if not grieved or handled well. The emotions and thoughts associated with loss must be given full expression and worked through to be fully grieved.

- The grieving process leads to acceptance. This takes time and cannot be hurried. Moving through pain, rather than avoiding it, brings closure.

- We cannot prevent all traumatic events from happening, but we can control how we respond to those memories mentally and emotionally.

Unfortunately, trauma, genetics, and difficult life experiences can become the foundation on which some people build a life of worry. We can cling to worry and choose to see the world in a worried way, or we can let God transform our thinking into a willing walk of faith.

WHAT ARE the Reasons We Worry?

Coping with their father's illness and its economic impact on the family business leaves our four siblings wading into deeper waters. Medical expenses mount and financial fears soar. How will they manage to navigate this uncharted territory? Each responds to these storms in their lives in different ways.

"This is a trustworthy saying.
And I want you to stress these things,
so that those who have trusted in God
may be careful to devote themselves
to doing what is good.
These things are excellent
and profitable for everyone."
Titus 3:8

▶ **Carefree Connie**

- Lives so much in the present that she neglects learning from the past and responsibly planning for the future: "Dad's mother had cancer and I know plenty of people who have cancer. Dad will be fine."

- Focuses on selfish desires or doing what she thinks is right: "I've still got a job and am bringing home a paycheck, so I'm fine."

- Lacks conviction that she has no worries, cares, or concerns: "I'm not concerned about the future and I'm not worried at all about Dad."

"So, if you think you are standing firm, be careful that you don't fall!" (1 Corinthians 10:12).

▶ **Controlling Travis**

- Suppresses unresolved problems in the past and seeks to control the future, so present opportunities are missed: "Even though my grandmother had cancer, I've done the research and Dad is getting the best medical care. I'll keep the business afloat for when he returns to work."

- Overcompensates for others' dysfunction and thus suffers from lack of joy: "My brother and sisters aren't much help, so I've got to hold the business and our family together."

- Needs to control situations and circumstances, and experiences exhaustion: "It doesn't matter how tired I am. I can manage the business and its finances by myself, because that's the only way I know things are getting done."

"Unless the Lord builds a house, the work of the builders is wasted. It is useless for you to work so hard from early morning until late at night, anxiously working for food to eat; for God gives rest to his loved ones" (Psalm 127:1–2 NLT).

▶ Consumed Susan

- Extreme fear in the past overwhelms the present and creates dread for the future: "Cancer took everything my grandmother had—and now it's going to take Dad, too!"

- Struggles with potential problems as much as actual issues, and lacks coping skills and a support system: "If the business goes under, then we'll all go bankrupt."

- Suffers from a lack of sleep, depression, and exhausts herself and others: "I spend every day and every night worrying. No one takes this as seriously as I do."

"Now you too have proved to be of no help; you see something dreadful and are afraid" (Job 6:21).

▶ Concerned Chris

- Learns from the past, lives in the present, plans appropriately for the future: "Even though my grandmother passed away from cancer, God may have a different path for Dad. We'll keep praying and walking along with him, one day at a time."

- Can develop a tendency to care too much, and be more focused on others rather than self: "I wish there was more I could do for Mom and Dad."

- Relies on God and eagerly helps others, but might ignore self-care and asking for help: "I'll keep trusting God for all of our needs."

"The LORD is my strength and shield. I trust him with all my heart. He helps me, and my heart is filled with joy" (Psalm 28:7 NLT).

Why Do We Worry?

We can list dozens of reasons why we worry. Like "Chicken Little," a character in a folktale with a moral message (known in parts of the world as "Henny Penny"), we can banty about the countryside crying out, "The sky is falling! The sky is falling!" And all because an acorn or a leaf once fell on our head.

How much of our worry directly relates to an unlikely or even non-existent threat? How often do we wrestle with "I wonder what …" and wile away our time with the "what-ifs" of life?

But consider one more "what-if" question: What if our worry directly relates to a lack of trust in God?

Even after seeing Jesus perform miracle after miracle, the disciples wonder and worry for their safety as they sail into the midst of a great windstorm. While Jesus sleeps in the boat's stern, the wind and waves threaten to sink the boat. But when the disciples wake Jesus, crying out, *"Teacher, don't you care?"* (Mark 4:38), He calms the troubled sea and then their troubled hearts, saying …

> "Why are you so afraid?
> Do you still have no faith?"
> Mark 4:10

Examine some of the reasons why we worry:

Distorted Thinking

Trusting God to save you for eternity but not trusting that He will meet your everyday needs in a way that will accomplish His purposes for your life.

"Which of you, if your son asks for bread, will give him a stone? Or if he asks for a fish, will give him a snake? If you, then, though you are evil, know how to give good gifts to your children, how much more will your Father in heaven give good gifts to those who ask him!" (Matthew 7:9–11).

Illusion of Control

Thinking that by mentally rearranging future events you can control the outcome.

"Now listen, you who say, 'Today or tomorrow we will go to this or that city, spend a year there, carry on business and make money.' Why, you do not even know what will happen tomorrow. What is your life? You are a mist that appears for a little while and then vanishes. Instead, you ought to say, 'If it is the Lord's will, we will live and do this or that'" (James 4:13–15).

Super Responsibility

Having a burdened sense of duty to make every area of your life perfect, not having learned to set your hope on the grace of God.

"With minds that are alert and fully sober, set your hope on the grace to be brought to you when Jesus Christ is revealed" (1 Peter 1:13).

Transferred Guilt

Allowing false guilt to surface as worry in other areas instead of confronting areas of real sin in your life.

"When I kept silent, my bones wasted away through my groaning all day long. For day and night your hand was heavy on me; my strength was sapped as in the heat of summer. Then I acknowledged my sin to you and did not cover up my iniquity. I said, 'I will confess my transgressions to the LORD'—and you forgave the guilt of my sin" (Psalm 32:3–5).

Runaway Emotions

Letting worry or fear have full control when you face difficulties instead of choosing to respond in the way Scripture teaches.

"I sought the LORD, and he answered me; he delivered me from all my fears" (Psalm 34:4).

Unhealthy Need

Feeling a desperate need to have the approval of others and worrying about how you look and present yourself, rather than seeking to please God.

"Am I now trying to win the approval of human beings, or of God? Or am I trying to please people? If I were still trying to please people, I would not be a servant of Christ" (Galatians 1:10).

SPIRITUAL Starvation

Trying to live on spiritual nourishment gleaned in the past, but starving for lack of present spiritual intimacy with God.

"Taste and see that the LORD is good; blessed is the one who takes refuge in him. ... The lions may grow weak and hungry, but those who seek the LORD lack no good thing" (Psalm 34:8, 10).

TRAMPLED Self-image

Lacking a sense of your value to God and His thoughts toward you, thus feeling powerless to cope with problems.

"How precious to me are your thoughts, God! How vast is the sum of them! Were I to count them, they would outnumber the grains of sand—when I awake, I am still with you" (Psalm 139:17–18).

In their book, *Why Worry? Conquering a Common Inclination,* authors James R. Beck and David T. Moore say, "Worry is a small trickle of fear that meanders through the mind until it cuts a channel into which all other thoughts are drained."[23] What a perfect picture of worry!

Much of our thinking involves what we say in our heads but never speak aloud. Thus, many of our worry patterns are based on common misbeliefs or assumptions that simply are not true. So, if you want to conquer the worry habit, you must learn to monitor these unspoken voices, silencing them with the truth.

To find freedom from your worry, repeat in your mind these words of Jesus ...

> **"You will know the truth,
> and the truth will set you free."**
> **John 8:32**

Rationalizations of Worriers[24]

▶ **Rationalization:** "I feel sure that what I'm worried about will happen."

The Truth: "Most of what I worry about rarely or never happens."

God's Truth: *"Trust in the Lord with all your heart; do not depend on your own understanding. Seek his will in all you do, and he will show you which path to take"* (Proverbs 3:5–6 NLT).

▶ **Rationalization:** "It makes sense to worry because terrible things happen to me all the time."

The Truth: "Looking back, I can see that terrible things have rarely happened to me."

God's Truth: *"Surely God is my salvation; I will trust and not be afraid. The Lord, the Lord himself, is my strength and my defense; he has become my salvation"* (Isaiah 12:2).

▶ **Rationalization:** "Worry helps to prepare me for what might happen."

The Truth: "The future is in God's hands, so there's no reason for me to worry about this."

God's Truth: *"Commit everything you do to the Lord. Trust him, and he will help you"* (Psalm 37:5 NLT).

▶ **Rationalization:** "If I worry about this, then maybe I can keep it from happening."

The Truth: "I do not control the future, God does, and I can trust His plan for my life."

God's Truth: *"'For I know the plans I have for you,' declares the Lord, 'plans to prosper you and not to harm you, plans to give you hope and a future'"* (Jeremiah 29:11).

▶ **Rationalization:** "Worrying is better than doing nothing about it."

The Truth: "Spending inordinate amounts of time worrying accomplishes nothing."

God's Truth: *"... pour out your hearts to him, for God is our refuge"* (Psalm 62:8).

When the Israelites made their escape after fleeing from Egypt, they experienced fear. First, they feared Pharaoh's army in hot pursuit. However, the Lord swept the Egyptians into the sea after miraculously parting the waters for the Israelites to pass.

The Israelites trusted the Lord briefly before their next challenge. They went from the abundance of water that saved them from Pharaoh to traveling for three days with no water to quench their thirst. The Israelites came to a place with bitter water and, again, the Lord miraculously provided for them by making the water fit to drink.

Next their stomachs growled with hunger while their words grumbled against the Lord. Tasting freedom wasn't enough to sustain them, so they feared starving in the desert. Once again, the Lord miraculously provided for them with bread from heaven—manna. He would provide their daily bread for a full forty years before they reached the promised land. No one had too little and no one had too much. (In fact, if they did gather more than they were instructed to collect, the next day they found it rotten and riddled with maggots.)

Likewise, God continues to meet our daily needs. He gives us just what we need each day. He won't load us down with more than we can handle today (with His help) and He won't expect us to carry the burdens of tomorrow today. So we don't have to live in fear. We don't have to be weighed down by the past or worry about living in dread of the future. We simply need to live each moment we have been given. Live today and remember: ***God was, God is, and God always will be with us and for us.***

> "'Holy, holy, holy
> is the Lord God Almighty,'
> who was, and is, and is to come."
> Revelation 4:8

Three Inner Needs

We all have three inner needs: love, significance, and security.[25]

▶ **Love**—To know that someone is unconditionally committed to our best interest.

"My command is this: Love each other as I have loved you" (John 15:12).

▶ **Significance**—To know that our lives have meaning and purpose.

"I cry out to God Most High, to God, who fulfills his purpose for me" (Psalm 57:2 ESV).

▶ **Security**—To feel accepted and a sense of belonging.

"Whoever fears the LORD has a secure fortress, and for their children it will be a refuge" (Proverbs 14:26).

What do our inner needs reveal about us and our relationship with God?

God did not create any person or position or any amount of power or possessions to meet our deepest needs. People fail us and self-effort also fails to meet our deepest needs. If a person or thing could meet all our needs, we wouldn't need God! Our inner needs draw us into a deeper dependence on Christ and remind us that only God can satisfy the longings of our hearts. The Lord brings people and circumstances into our lives as an extension of His care, but ultimately only He can satisfy all the needs of our hearts.

The Bible says …

> "The LORD will guide you always;
> he will satisfy your needs in a sun-scorched
> land and will strengthen your frame.
> You will be like a well-watered garden,
> like a spring whose waters never fail."
> Isaiah 58:11

All along, the Lord planned to meet our deepest needs for …

▶ **Love**—*"I [the Lord] have loved you with an everlasting love; I have drawn you with unfailing kindness"* (Jeremiah 1:3).

▶ **Significance**—*"'For I know the plans I have for you,' declares the Lord, 'plans to prosper you and not to harm you, plans to give you hope and a future'"* (Jeremiah 29:11).

61

▶ **Security**—*"The* L ORD *himself goes before you and will be with you; he will never leave you nor forsake you. Do not be afraid; do not be discouraged"* (Deuteronomy 31:8).

Our needs for love, significance, and security can be legitimately met in Christ Jesus! Philippians 4:19 makes it plain ...

> "My God will meet all your needs
> according to the riches of his glory
> in Christ Jesus."

Although Jesus tells us not to worry, He understands our struggles. He does not judge or condemn what may seem to be a lack of faith on our part. Rather, Jesus admonishes and encourages us to take a step toward deeper faith by examining the misbeliefs we have about worry and exchanging our doubts and fears for the hope, love, joy, and peace He offers.

> "The Holy Spirit produces this kind of fruit
> in our lives: love, joy, peace, patience,
> kindness, goodness, faithfulness,
> gentleness, and self-control."
> Galatians 5:22–23 NLT

▶ **W RONG B ELIEF**—"I believe God cares about me, but I can't believe He is concerned with the everyday details of my life. I can't help but worry."

▶ **R IGHT B ELIEF**—"God has already promised to provide all the needs in my life through Christ. I don't need to worry about how He will carry out that promise. I will trust Him to do it."

Many worriers struggle with trust—especially trusting God. Most people begin basing their understanding on who God is by looking to the authority figures in their lives, starting with their parents. Woundedness from the past can distort our image of God.

▶ If you grew up in an abusive home, you may see God as absent or uncaring since He could have, but didn't, prevent the abuse.

▶ If you grew up with controlling parents, your perception of God may be as a manipulative puppet master.

▶ If you were a child of hypercritical parents, you might think of God as being disappointed in you or judgmental of you.

▶ Children who experience the loss of a parent may struggle to find comfort and security in our heavenly Father.

Sadly, no one grows up with perfect parents who are the ideal example of God's love and grace. But God longs to re-parent us if we will let Him into our hearts and lives. Even if we didn't have an ideal childhood or we've lived through many of life's storms, we can look to God who always proves Himself to be loving, faithful, and worthy of our trust.

To rid yourself of worry, you must first acknowledge that God is the creator of your life. He wants to be your provider and protector. God has a vested interest in your well-being because He made you and He loves you.

Next, you must submit your will and your worries to God's control. When He is in control, you don't have to *worry* about anything. In fact, don't worry about your future. God is already there! When you trust in God, you can trust in His plan for your future.

> "There is surely a future hope for you,
> and your hope will not be cut off."
> Proverbs 23:18

Four Points of God's Plan

Whether you're trying to make sense of your past, trying to overcome something in the present, or trying to make changes for a better future, the Lord cares about you. He loves you. No matter what challenges you or your loved ones are facing, no matter the pain or difficult feelings you may be experiencing, no matter what you've done or what's been done to you, there is hope. And that hope is found in Jesus Christ.

God has a plan for your life, and it begins with a personal relationship with Jesus. The most important decision you can ever make is whether you will receive His invitation. If you have never made that decision, these four simple truths can help you start your journey together with Him.

> "'For I know the plans I have for you,'
> declares the LORD,
> 'plans to prosper you and not to harm you,
> plans to give you hope and a future.'"
> Jeremiah 29:11

1. **God's Purpose for You Is *Salvation*.**

What was God's motivation in sending Jesus Christ to earth?

To express His love for you by saving you!

The Bible says, *"God so loved the world that he gave his one and only Son, that whoever believes in him shall not perish but have eternal life. For God did not send his Son into the world to condemn the world, but to save the world through him"* (John 3:16–17).

What was Jesus' purpose in coming to earth?

To forgive your sins, to empower you to have victory over sin, and to enable you to live a fulfilled life!

Jesus said, *"I have come that they may have life, and have it to the full"* (John 10:10).

2. **The Problem Is *Sin*.**

What exactly is sin?

Sin is living independently of God's standard—knowing what is wrong and doing it anyway—also knowing what is right and choosing not to do it.

The apostle Paul said, *"I know that nothing good lives in me, that is, in my sinful nature. I want to do what is right, but I can't. I want to do what is good, but I don't. I don't want to do what is wrong, but I do it anyway"* (Romans 7:18–19 NLT).

What is the major consequence of sin?

Spiritual death, eternal separation from God.

The Bible says, *"Your iniquities [sins] have separated you from your God"* (Isaiah 59:2).

Scripture also says, *"The wages of sin is death, but the gift of God is eternal life in Christ Jesus our Lord"* (Romans 6:23).

3. God's Provision for You Is *the Savior.*

Can anything remove the penalty for sin?

Yes! Jesus died on the cross to personally pay the penalty for your sins.

The Bible says, *"God demonstrates his own love for us in this: While we were still sinners, Christ died for us"* (Romans 5:8).

What is the solution to being separated from God?

Belief in (entrusting your life to) Jesus Christ as the only way to God the Father.

Jesus said, *"I am the way and the truth and the life. No one comes to the Father except through me"* (John 14:6).

The Bible says, *"Believe in the Lord Jesus, and you will be saved"* (Acts 16:31).

4. Your Part Is *Surrender.*

Give Christ control of your life, entrusting yourself to Him.

Jesus said, *"Whoever wants to be my disciple must deny themselves and take up their cross and follow me. For whoever wants to save their life will lose it, but whoever loses their life for me will find it. What good will it be for someone to gain the whole world, yet forfeit their soul?"* (Matthew 16:24–26).

Place your faith in (rely on) Jesus Christ as your personal Lord and Savior and reject your "good works" as a means of earning God's approval.

The Bible says, *"It is by grace you have been saved, through faith—and this is not from yourselves, it is the gift of God—not by works, so that no one can boast"* (Ephesians 2:8–9).

Has there been a time in your life when you know you've humbled your heart and received Jesus Christ as your personal Lord and Savior—giving Him control of your life? You can tell God that you want to surrender your life to Christ in a simple, heartfelt prayer like this:

PRAYER OF SALVATION

"God, I want a real relationship with you.
I admit that many times
I've chosen to go my own way
instead of your way.
Please forgive me for my sins.
Jesus, thank you for dying on the cross
to pay the penalty for my sins.
Come into my life to be my Lord
and my Savior.
Change me from the inside out
and make me the person
you created me to be.
In your holy name I pray. Amen."

What Can You Now Expect?

When you surrender your life to Christ, you receive the Holy Spirit who empowers you to live a life pleasing to God.

The Bible says, *"His divine power has given us everything we need for a godly life"* (2 Peter 1:3).

Jesus assures those who believe with these words ...

> "Truly I tell you, whoever hears my word
> and believes him who sent me
> has eternal life and will not be judged
> but has crossed over from death to life."
> John 5:24

STEPS TO SOLUTION

Imagine never worrying about anything. Not one thing. Not on the job, not in your home, not at school, in your city, town, or neighborhood—not even in the world. Does this seem impossible? It isn't. And here's why: God knows. Although you can't see Him, God is watching over you and cares about every detail of your life as Hebrews 4:13 declares, *"Nothing in all creation is hidden from God's sight."* No matter what issue you are facing, God knows. He is the all-knowing, all-caring Father who is intimately invested in your life and knows what you need even before you do.

Are you worried about an upcoming medical procedure or surgery? God knows. Trust Him. Are you worried about your job or a performance review coming up? God knows. Rest in Him. Are you worried about your children or grandchildren? God knows. Release them to Him.

When Jesus told His followers not to worry or fret about anything, He wasn't simply making a spiritually sound suggestion or leaving room for theological "yeah-buts." He was giving them a straightforward command. The apostle Paul echoes Jesus' words in his letter to the Philippian believers, immediately after which he instructs them: *"Instead of worrying, pray"* (Philippians 4:6 MSG).

Do you want to worry less? Pray more. Take your worries to God. Pour out your concerns, your fears, your cares to Him. Tell Him what is keeping you awake at night. If you will do this, God promises to guard your mind (thoughts) and your heart (feelings) with His peace, a peace that comes from knowing He is in control.

As you learn to trust Him more and more, may these words from Scripture prove true for you …

"Grace and peace be yours in abundance
through the knowledge of God
and of Jesus our Lord."
2 Peter 1:2

A sign in front of a church read, "When your knees knock together, kneel on them."[26] That's good advice. In fact, that's just the godly advice the apostle Paul gave the church at Philippi when he wrote encouraging them to turn their worries into prayers.

KEY VERSES TO MEMORIZE

"Don't fret or worry.
Instead of worrying, pray.
Let petitions and praises
shape your worries into prayers,
letting God know your concerns.
Before you know it,
a sense of God's wholeness,
everything coming together for good,
will come and settle you down.
It's wonderful what happens when Christ
displaces worry at the center of your life."
Philippians 4:6–7 MSG

Key Passage to Read

When Jesus gave words of warning and encouragement to His disciples regarding worry and fretfulness, He essentially told them that worrying is worthless, anxiousness is aggravating, and fretting is fruitless. We need only look at the world around us to see how good God the Father is to His creation—even to the extent of feeding the birds of the air and clothing the flowers of the field.

When we realize the kingdom of God is our guaranteed inheritance, we have nothing to worry about—nothing to be anxious about. Our future is entirely and eternally secure.

> "Do not be afraid, little flock. Your Father is pleased to give you the kingdom."
> Luke 12:32 GW

Luke 12:22–34

If you worry about life, then God says to you …

▶ You are forgetting that life is about more than what you need to live. (v. 22)

▶ You are missing the deeper meaning of life. (v. 23)

▶ You are forgetting that you are far more important to Me than the birds and flowers which I lavishly take care of. (v. 24)

▶ You cannot add even a single minute to your life by worrying about it. (v. 25)

▶ You are engaging in an exercise that is utterly unproductive. (v. 26)

▶ You are not taking into consideration how I clothe the grass of the fields with flowers more splendid than even Solomon's clothes. (v. 27)

▶ You must grow in faith—trust Me completely, depend on Me fully to provide for you. (v. 28)

▶ You are setting your heart on the wrong things— on tangible things I will provide. (v. 29)

▶ You are acting like unbelievers who run after such things rather than depend on Me. (v. 30)

▶ You are not to worry about security and safety, about food and clothing, but rather to pursue My Kingdom and trust Me to give you all that you need. (v. 31)

▶ You do not need to be afraid of "missing out" because the Father wants to give you the very kingdom itself. (v. 32)

▶ You are to use your earthly possessions to help others and, in doing so, you will store up treasure in heaven forever. (v. 33)

▶ You are to stay consciously aware that your heart will be where your treasure is. (v. 34)

God's Sovereignty

QUESTION: "How does the fact that God is sovereign help me overcome fear and worry?"

ANSWER: The word *sovereign* means that God is absolutely free to do whatever He chooses. But you must understand this within the context of His character. For instance, because God is completely holy, it is impossible for Him to sin. So whatever He decides to do will always be perfectly holy, perfectly just, perfectly loving, and perfectly wise.

When you're filled with worry—when it feels like your life is coming apart at the seams—the truth that God is sovereign will bring you hope, peace, and confidence. The knowledge that God is in control (He is sovereign) can calm your greatest fear and wash away your most consuming worry.

When worry threatens to overwhelm you, remember these key truths about God's sovereignty:[27]

▶ **He controls** every event, every outcome in life. (Personalize that!)

"The LORD determines every outcome" (Proverbs 16:33 GW).

▶ **He is keenly aware** of what happens in nature itself, determining the seasons, the weather, and the growth of crops.

"Rejoice in the LORD your God, for he has given you the autumn rains because he is faithful. He sends you abundant showers, both autumn and spring rains" (Joel 2:23).

▶ **He determines** exactly how long each of us will live.

"You have decided the length of our lives. You know how many months we will live, and we are not given a minute longer" (Job 14:5 NLT).

▶ **He is completely free** to do whatever He chooses.

"God is one of a kind. Who can make him change his mind? He does whatever he wants" (Job 23:13 GW).

▶ **He is sovereign** over everything—even our sin, rebellion, and foolishness.

"You intended to harm me, but God intended it for good to accomplish what is now being done, the saving of many lives" (Genesis 50:20).

HOW TO Have a Transformed Life

Followers of Christ aren't immune to worry or its complications. We want family, friends, neighbors, and coworkers to see us trusting in the goodness and provision of God. Yet, we worry about letting them down or whether or not our faith will make an impact on their lives.

The consequences of worry are costly. It divides our attention and saps our energy. We don't know what to do with the cares and concerns that wear us down. When we are preoccupied with what *might* happen, we let worry superimpose a negative future outcome on a current situation.

Our challenge as believers is to learn what God has given us to help deal with wily worries, step out in faith, and through His empowering Spirit, make life changes.

"Don't be afraid,
because the Lord your God
will be with you everywhere you go."
Joshua 1:9 NCV

REACHING THE TARGET: TRANSFORMATION!

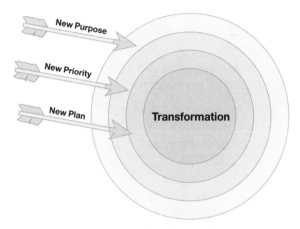

THE FREEDOM FORMULA

	A New Purpose
+	A New Priority
+	A New Plan

A Transformed Life

Target 1—A New Purpose: God's purpose for me is to be conformed to the character of Christ.

> *"Those God foreknew he also predestined to be conformed to the image of his Son"* (Romans 8:29).

- "I'll do whatever it takes to be conformed to the character of Christ."

Target 2—A New Priority: God's priority for me is to change my thinking.

> *"Do not conform to the pattern of this world, but be transformed by the renewing of your mind"* (Romans 12:2).

- "I'll do whatever it takes to line up my thinking with God's thinking."

Target 3—A New Plan: God's plan for me is to rely on Christ's strength, not my strength, to be all He created me to be.

"I can do all things through Christ who strengthens me" (Philippians 4:13 NKJV).

- "I'll do whatever it takes to fulfill His plan in His strength."

My Personalized Plan

Worries become well-rehearsed words swirling around in my mind. I know I shouldn't worry, but I can't seem to stop the worrisome words, then I worry about worrying! Fortunately, God doesn't simply say, "Stop worrying," without telling me *how* to stop worrying. If I want my worries to vanish, then I must learn new ways of thinking and develop methods for changing my former thinking patterns. Although my thoughts and memories may not be erased, the rehearsed words can be replaced as I focus on the wisdom of Philippians 4:6–9.

> [6] *"Do not be anxious about anything, but in every situation, by prayer and petition, with thanksgiving, present your requests to God.* [7] *And the peace of God, which transcends all understanding, will guard your hearts and your minds in Christ Jesus.* [8] *Finally, brothers and sisters, whatever is true, whatever is noble, whatever is right, whatever is pure, whatever is lovely, whatever is admirable—if anything is*

excellent or praiseworthy—think about such things. ⁹ *Whatever you have learned or received or heard from me, or seen in me—put it into practice. And the God of peace will be with you."*
Philippians 4:6–9

Applying God's Word to My Worry

As I seek to overcome worry in my life on a daily basis, I will personally apply the truths of God's Word found in Philippians 4:6–9.

▷ **I will choose** not to worry or be anxious about anything. (v. 6)

▷ **I will bring** every situation that concerns me to God rather than worrying about it. (v. 6)

▷ **I will tell** God what I need, and thank Him for all He's done for me. (v. 6)

▷ **I will focus** on having a heart of praise and thankfulness. (v. 6)

▷ **I will let** His peace guard all of my thoughts and feelings—my entire mind and heart. (v. 7)

▷ **I will direct** my thoughts, intentionally fixing them on what is true, honorable, right, pure, lovely, admirable, excellent, and praiseworthy. (v. 8)

▷ **I will act** in a way that reflects God—His words, His teachings, His actions, His character, His example in thought, word, and deed. (v. 9)

▷ **I will continually remember** that the God of peace will be with me *always.* (v. 9)

As I seek to overcome worry by applying God's Word to my life, I will also commit to applying it God's *way* and in His strength. Therefore, I will …

▶ **Acknowledge** what I worry about.

- Honestly evaluate the people or situations that burden me.

- Make a "Worry List" of my concerns, detailing each one and the outcome I hope to ultimately see.

"Oh, that my words were recorded, that they were written on a scroll" (Job 19:23).

▶ **Read** Philippians 4:8 carefully, one point at a time.

- Evaluate my fretful thoughts against each point in Philippians 4:8.

- Ask myself, "Are my thoughts true? Noble? Right? Pure? Lovely? Admirable? Excellent? Praiseworthy?"

"Whatever is true, whatever is noble, whatever is right, whatever is pure, whatever is lovely, whatever is admirable—if anything is excellent or praiseworthy— think about such things" (Philippians 4:8).

▶ **Present** each worry on my list to God, along with the details, moving all of them from my "Worry List" to my "Prayer List."

- Set aside a sufficient amount of time to present my requests to God.

- Pray, "Lord, I know you are fully aware of my situation regarding [the problem]. I am feeling [describe my emotions]. I want your will to be done in my life and in the lives of everyone involved. I relinquish control of this situation and thank you that you already have a resolution in mind. I am trusting you to reveal your will for me in your time and in your way. And I am relying on you to direct my course of action and guard my heart and mind. I will not worry about this anymore, but will continue to leave it in your hands. Thank you, Lord."

"I call on you, my God, for you will answer me; turn your ear to me and hear my prayer" (Psalm 17:6).

▶ **Slow** down my thinking.

- Become more aware of the thoughts rushing through my mind as they occur.

- Recognize my troubling thoughts, submit them to the scrutiny of God's Word, and write down their corrections. To change a thought, I must first capture it.

"We demolish arguments and every pretension that sets itself up against the knowledge of God, and we take captive every thought to make it obedient to Christ" (2 Corinthians 10:5).

▶ **Challenge** my mistaken or false beliefs. (Mistaken beliefs are at the core of worry.)

- Carry a notebook with me to capture and record thoughts that imply some belief that may be false.

- Write down why I know what I believe is mistaken or not true. Example: "I am a victim of the way others have treated me." "Not true. I can take control of my life now and change the outcome."

"Be joyful in hope, patient in affliction, faithful in prayer" (Romans 12:12).

▶ **Change** my focus from *worrying* to *resting* in God's sovereignty.

- I will recite scriptures that remind me of God's sovereign rule over my life.

- I will sing and listen to songs that focus on the faithfulness of God and His character, and practice resting in Him by remembering and focusing on His goodness and faithfulness.

"Return to your rest, my soul, for the LORD has been good to you" (Psalm 116:7).

HOW TO Correct Faulty Thinking

In his book, *The Dance of Hope*, Bill Frey recalls a day from his childhood in Georgia.[28] At age eleven, one of his chores was to gather firewood. Young Bill would search for tree stumps to chop into kindling. Saturated with resin, pine wood burned easily and one large stump caught Bill's attention. But to Bill's surprise, the stump had a strong, deep root system. After hours of trying every trick and tool he could think of, Bill was no closer to pulling up that stubborn stump.

Bill was still struggling with the stump when his father returned home from work. Spying his son, he went over to watch. "I think I see your problem," he said. "What's that?" Bill asked. "You're not using all your strength," he replied. This lit a fuse in Bill's young heart and he proceeded to tell his dad just how long and hard he had been working! "No," his father said, "you're not using all your strength." Later, Bill calmed down and asked his father what he meant. His father replied, "You haven't asked me to help you yet."

Likewise, we don't access the strength available to us by going to our heavenly Father when we face a seemingly insurmountable problem. When worries wear you down, you need a plan of action. Rather than retreat in defeat, understand your core beliefs and why you worry. Examine your heart and seek the Lord's help to correct your faulty thinking.

> "Your Father knows what you need
> before you ask him."
> Matthew 6:8

A Breakthrough Battle Plan[29]

When worry woes leave you weary, remember that God can shed light on our darkest moments. Even in the pain and anguish of what seems to be a breakdown, God can deliver a breakthrough to hope and victory.

▶ **Acknowledge your feelings when you worry.**

- Your feelings are not haphazard or free-floating, but rather connected to your thoughts and perceptions.

- You matter and your feelings matter, too.

- Your feelings help you gauge the healthiness and helpfulness of your thoughts.

- When your feelings become overwhelming and you are overcome with emotion, know that something you may have repressed is bubbling up from deep within.

- Your feelings are useful in revealing the degree of impact an event had on you.

▶ **Avoid the five *B*s of worry.**

#1 *Busyness:* Martha worried about all the work she had to do while Mary spent time listening to Jesus (Luke 10:38–42).

#2 *Blaming:* Adam and Eve blamed each other, blamed the serpent, and ultimately blamed God for their disobedience (Genesis 3:12–13).

#3 *Bingeing:* The prodigal son demanded, then squandered, his inheritance on wild living (Luke 15:11–31).

#4 *Burying:* Pharaoh delayed releasing the Israelites (Exodus 5); Jonah avoided preaching to the Ninevites (Jonah 1:1–3); and Peter denied knowing Jesus (Luke 22:61).

#5 *Brooding:* King Saul brooded over David's success and popularity (1 Samuel 18:7–8).

▶ **Address the worries.**

- Is this a legitimate concern or an illegitimate worry?

- How likely is it that a particular event will actually happen?

- Is there evidence that what you're worrying about is an actual risk?

- If there is a risk, how much control do you have over it?

- What will you plan to do if the thing you are worrying about occurs?

▶ **Ask for help.**

- Acknowledge your struggle.

- Admit you need help.

- Ask the Lord to help you.

- Accept the answer.

- Align your request with the character of God and His promises.

▶ **Attack the issue.**

- Don't get stuck in unhealthy thought patterns.

- Be brave. It won't be easy, but you can do it with the Lord's help.

- Fight the fear. Remember you are not alone in this battle.

- Pray Philippians 4:6–9.

- Trust in the Lord's faithfulness on a day-to-day basis.

Don't let your desire to be in control become a testimony to a lack of faith in God's ability to take care of you. Don't make it your job to do His job. Live like you believe in Him, what He can do, and what He will do for you.

> "In all my prayers for all of you,
> I always pray with joy
> … being confident of this,
> that he who began a good work in you
> will carry it on to completion
> until the day of Christ Jesus."
> **Philippians 1:4, 6**

WHAT IS the Two-step Solution to Worry?

If you had to boil down all efforts to manage worry to the most essential basic steps, you could reduce the solution to two steps: one *ask* and one *action* step.

▶ **Step 1. Ask**: Can I change this situation that I am worried about?

▶ **Step 2. Action:** If you can change it now, *then change it*. If you can't, release it and allow God to take care of the situation and you.

Let's review the first step: Right now, can you change what worries you? Answer *yes* or *no*—that's it.

Now consider the second step: If you answered *yes*, and you are worried about something you can change, then change it.

- If the door squeaks, oil it.

- If the faucet leaks, fix it.

   If you fear losing your job, your home, your financial security, your spouse, your children, your friends—even your very life—and there is something you can do besides worry, then do it! Give your employer your best effort, manage your home and finances well, love your parents, your spouse, your children and friends, but resist the temptation to worry.

If you answered *no,* you are worrying about something you cannot change. Then let it go and allow God to take care of it and you.

- If you fear suffering a loss in the future, let it go (the fear). If you fear losing your job, your home, your financial security, your spouse, your children, your friends, even your very life, worrying about it will not change the situation. It will only make matters worse.

- If you worry over what might happen in the future, let God be in control—because He already is!

How do you let go of worry? First, identify what worries you—every issue, every situation. Then, go to God in all humility and surrender the situation and yourself to the Lord—past, present, and future. Although you may feel completely powerless, in reality you have the power to release your worry to Him.

"RELEASING YOUR WORRY" PRAYER

"Lord Jesus, thank you for loving me.
Thank you for caring about me.
Since you know everything, you know
the strong sense of fear and worry
I have felt about [name or situation].
Thank you for understanding
my worry and forgiving me
when I struggle with avoidance
and seek control through worry.
Right now, I release all of my worry to you.
I trust you with my future and myself.
In Jesus' name, Amen."

Weathering the storms of life, our quartet of siblings comes to realize that although they've had ups and downs in their lives, they don't have to fall for the enemy's tactics bent on doom and destruction. When seeds of mistrust are sown, they don't have to tend the garden of despair and reap the weeds of worry.

Even when they face future storms in life, they rest in the assurance that God is in control … and they don't have to be. Whenever the enemy wants to steal their joy with worries, God wants to bless them with His peace. Relying on Jesus through His presence and provision, He will replace worries with joy.

> "You will show me the path of life;
> In Your presence is fullness of joy;
> At Your right hand are pleasures
> forevermore."
> **Psalm 16:11** NKJV

▶ **Carefree Connie**

- Learns appropriate levels of care and concern for herself: "Because God sees me as worthy of care and concern, I should see myself through His eyes."

- Develops healthy care and concern for others: "I can stop avoiding scary situations and start showing how much I really do care for others."

- Realizes the challenges of life are worthy of care and concern: "The blessings of living life are worth the risks of loving others."

"Do everything in love" (1 Corinthians 16:14).

▶ Controlling Travis

- Trusts God because He is sovereign and He cares: "I don't have to be in control of everything because, honestly, I'm not in control. God is."

- Doesn't carry the weight of the world on his shoulders, and seeks and finds rest: "I don't have to do everything, just what God has called me to do. I can rest in His promises."

- Learns to share the burdens of life and seeks help from others: "Instead of carrying all the responsibility, I can ask others for help by sharing the load and revealing what I've learned."

"Carry each other's burdens, and in this way you will fulfill the law of Christ" (Galatians 6:2).

▶ Consumed Susan

- Trusts God and understands that change is possible: "When I focus on my problems, I lose sight of God. I know He can change my perspective and my outlook."

- Sets boundaries for life in general and thoughts in particular: "If I start to fall into the worry trap, I will turn to God and His Word to redirect my thoughts."

- Shifts thinking from gloom and doom to hope and help: "I don't have to battle this alone. I can seek the wise counsel of others."

"With us is the LORD our God to help us and to fight our battles" (2 Chronicles 32:8).

▶ Concerned Chris

- Maintains healthy spiritual life and relationships: "I need to rely on the Lord to help me balance my life in ways that keep me connected to what's important."

- Refrains from dealing with worries in an unhealthy manner: "If my thoughts start to slip into worry, I will turn those worrisome thoughts into a prayer."

- Doesn't neglect his own needs: "I will remember that I can't give away something I don't have, so I will do my best to make sure my mind stays centered in a healthy place of spiritual strength. Then, I can help others."

"It is God who arms me with strength and keeps my way secure" (2 Samuel 22:33).

▶ **If You Say:** "I'm afraid my situation is impossible."

The Lord Says: I can make all things possible.

"What is impossible with man is possible with God" (Luke 18:27).

▶ **If You Say:** "I feel worried over the cares of the world."

The Lord Says: Cast all your cares on Me.

"Cast your cares on the LORD and he will sustain you" (Psalm 55:22).

▶ **If You Say:** "I'm overwhelmed with fear."

The Lord Says: I will give you My strength when you're afraid.

"Do not fear, for I am with you; do not be dismayed, for I am your God. I will strengthen you and help you; I will uphold you with my righteous right hand" (Isaiah 41:10).

▶ **If You Say:** "I'm so worried—I can't forgive myself."

The Lord Says: I can forgive you.

"If we confess our sins, he is faithful and just and will forgive us our sins and purify us from all unrighteousness" (1 John 1:9).

▶ **If You Say:** "I'm worried that my loved ones might leave me."

The Lord Says: Once you've come to Me, I will never leave you.

"The L<small>ORD</small> himself goes before you and will be with you; he will never leave you nor forsake you. Do not be afraid; do not be discouraged" (Deuteronomy 31:8).

▶ **If You Say:** "I'm worried about death."

The Lord Says: I will give you eternal life.

"For God so loved the world that he gave his one and only Son, that whoever believes in him shall not perish but have eternal life" (John 3:16).

▶ **If You Say:** "I'm so worried that I can't rest."

The Lord Says: I will give you my rest.

"Are you tired? Worn out? Burned out on religion? Come to me. Get away with me and you'll recover your life. I'll show you how to take a real rest. Walk with me and work with me—watch how I do it. Learn the unforced rhythms of grace. I won't lay anything heavy or ill-fitting on you. Keep company with me and you'll learn to live freely and lightly" (Matthew 11:28–30 M<small>SG</small>).

> When worries sprout, weed them out.
> Don't fret over the future—
> God is already there.
>
> —J<small>UNE</small> H<small>UNT</small>

SCRIPTURES TO MEMORIZE

Where can I find **peace** and **safety** so I can **sleep**?

*"In **peace** I will lie down and **sleep**, for you alone, LORD, make me dwell in **safety**"* (Psalm 4:8).

If I am **not anxious about anything**, will I have **peace**, and will that peace **guard** my **heart and** my **mind**?

*"Do **not** be **anxious about anything**, but in every situation, by prayer and petition, with thanksgiving, present your requests to God. And the **peace** of God, which transcends all understanding, will **guard** your **hearts and** your **minds** in Christ Jesus"* (Philippians 4:6–7).

How can I **not worry about tomorrow**—even though I know that **each day has enough trouble of its own**?

*"Do **not worry about tomorrow**, for tomorrow will worry about itself. **Each day has enough trouble of its own**"* (Matthew 6:34).

What keeps **hearts** from being **weighed down** by the **anxieties of life**?

*"Be careful, or your **hearts** will be **weighed down** with … the **anxieties of life**"* (Luke 21:34).

Will I be **blessed** if I **trust in the Lord** and put my **confidence in Him**?

*"**Blessed** is the one who **trusts in the LORD**, whose **confidence** is **in him**"* (Jeremiah 17:7).

Who is **my strength** and **my shield**, in whom **my heart trusts** and I find **joy**?

*"The L*ORD *is **my strength** and **my shield**; **my heart trusts** in him, and he helps me. My heart leaps for **joy**, and with my song I praise him"* (Psalm 28:7).

In whom can **I trust** for **shelter** and **rest**?

*"Whoever dwells in the **shelter** of the Most High will **rest** in the shadow of the Almighty. I will say of the L*ORD*, 'He is my refuge and my fortress, my God, in whom **I trust**'"* (Psalm 91:1–2).

Who has **answered** and **delivered me from all my fears**?

*"I sought the L*ORD*, and he **answered** me; he **delivered me from all my fears**"* (Psalm 34:4).

Who replaces my worries with **hope**, **joy**, and **peace**?

*"May the God of **hope** fill you with all **joy** and **peace** as you trust in him"* (Romans 15:13).

Who is **my help**, the **one who sustains me**?

*"Surely God is **my help**; the L*ORD *is the **one who sustains me**"* (Psalm 54:4).

NOTES

1   *Merriam-Webster Online Dictionary*, s.v. "worry," accessed June 13, 2019, http://www.merriam-webster.com/dictionary/worry.

2   Linda Mintle, PhD, *Letting Go of Worry: God's Plan for Finding Peace and Contentment* (Eugene, OR: Harvest House Publishers, 2011), 19.

3   For English translation of *wurgen*, see https://dictionary.reverso.net/german-english/wurgen, accessed June 13, 2019.

4   W. E. Vine, M. A. Merrill F. Unger, ThM, ThD, PhD, & Williams White, Jr., ThM, PhD, *Expository Dictionary of Biblical Words* (Nashville, TN: Thomas Nelson, 1984), 160.

5   James Strong, *A Concise Dictionary of the Words in the Greek Testament and The Hebrew Bible*, s.v. "divide," #G3307.

6   Vine, *Expository Dictionary of Biblical Words*, 86.

7   Max Lucado, *Less Fret More Faith: An 11-week Action Plan to Overcome Anxiety* (Nashville, TN: Thomas Nelson Publishers, 2017), vi.

8   Lucado, *Less Fret More Faith*, vii. (Lucado's exact quote, adapted here, is: "Fear sees a threat. Anxiety imagines one.")

9   American Psychiatric Association, *Diagnostic and Statistical Manual of Mental Disorders*, 5th edition, text revision (Washington, D.C.: American Psychiatric Association, 2013), 189; Abigail Powers Lott, PhD, and Anais Stenson, PhD, *"Types of Anxiety,"* Anxiety: anxiety.org (June 17, 2019).

10 Dictionary.com, s.v. "concern," accessed June 14, 2019, https://www.dictionary.com/browse/concern.

11 Etymonline.com, (n.) "concern," accessed June 15, 2019, https://www.etymonline.com/word/concern#etymonline_v_17308.

12 Mintle, *Letting Go of Worry*, 20.

13 William Backus, *The Good News about Worry* (Minneapolis, MN: Bethany House Publishers, 1991), 14–15.

14 Backus, *The Good News about Worry,* 14–15.

15 Archibald D. Hart, PhD, *The Anxiety Cure: You Can Find Emotional Tranquility and Wholeness* (Nashville, TN: Thomas Nelson, 1999), 156.

16 Mintle, *Letting Go of Worry*, 20–22.

17 David Stoop, PhD, *Self Talk: Key to Personal Growth* (Grand Rapids, MI: Fleming H. Revell, 1982), 94.

18 Backus, *The Good News about Worry*, 23–24.

19 Mintle, *Letting Go of Worry*, 24.

20 Mintle, *Letting Go of Worry*, 29–39.

21 Melinda Beck, "When Fretting Is in Your DNA: Overcoming the Worry Gene," *Wall Street Journal*, January 15, 2008, online edition, http:online.wsj.com/articles/SB120035993435490045. html, as cited in Dr. Linda Mintle's book, *Letting Go of Worry*, 30. Article no longer available online.

22 Mintle, *Letting Go of Worry*, 30.

23 James R. Beck and David T. Moore, *Why Worry? Conquering a Common Inclination* (Grand Rapids, MI: Baker Books, 1994), 42.

24 Beck and Moore, *Why Worry?*, 45–47.

25 Lawrence J. Crabb, Jr., *Understanding People: Why We Long for Relationship* (Grand Rapids, MI: Zondervan, 2013), 17–18, 124–127; Robert S. McGee, *The Search for Significance: Seeing Your True Worth through God's Eyes*, rev. ed. (Nashville, TN: Thomas Nelson, 2003), 6–11, 21–24.

26 Wolfgang Mieder, ed., *A Dictionary of American Proverbs* (New York, NY: Oxford University Press, 1992), 585

27 Elyse Fitzpatrick, *Overcoming Fear, Worry, and Anxiety* (Eugene, OR: Harvest House Publishers, 2001), 127–128.

28 William C. Frey, *The Dance of Hope: Finding Ourselves in the Rhythm of God's Great Story* (Colorado Springs, CO: WaterBrook Press, 2003), 175.

29 Alli Worthington, *Fierce Faith: A Woman's Guide to Fighting Fear, Wrestling Worry, and Overcoming Anxiety* (Grand Rapids, MI: Zondervan, 2018), 43–46; 144–146; 182–183.

HOPE FOR THE HEART TITLES

- *Adultery*
- *Aging Well*
- *Alcohol & Drug Abuse*
- *Anger*
- *Anorexia & Bulimia*
- *Anxiety*
- *Boundaries*
- *Bullying*
- *Caregiving*
- *Chronic Illness & Disability*
- *Codependency*
- *Conflict Resolution*
- *Confrontation*
- *Considering Marriage*
- *Critical Spirit*
- *Decision Making*
- *Depression*
- *Domestic Violence*
- *Dysfunctional Family*
- *Envy & Jealousy*
- *Fear*
- *Financial Freedom*
- *Forgiveness*
- *Friendship*
- *Gambling*
- *Grief*
- *Guilt*
- *Hope*
- *Loneliness*
- *Manipulation*
- *Marriage*
- *Overeating*
- *Parenting*
- *Perfectionism*
- *Procrastination*
- *Reconciliation*
- *Rejection*
- *Self-Worth*
- *Sexual Integrity*
- *Singleness*
- *Spiritual Abuse*
- *Stress*
- *Success Through Failure*
- *Suicide Prevention*
- *Trials*
- *Verbal & Emotional Abuse*
- *Victimization*
- *Worry*

www.hendricksonrose.com